Author: Henry Beaumont

ISBN HARDBACK: 978-9916-90-636-1

ISBN PAPERBACK: 978-9916-90-637-8

Flickering Lights of Distant Stars

In the velvet cloak of night,
Flickering lights begin to share,
Whispers of worlds far from sight,
Glowing softly in the air.

They dance like dreams across the sky,
Each a story yet untold,
Guiding seekers, low and high,
With mysteries to behold.

Distance wraps them, thin and bright,
Echoing ancient, timeless tales,
Woven deep in cosmic light,
Where imagination sails.

In the silence, hearts abide,
Finding hope in twinkling gleam,
Flickering stars, our dreams inside,
Illuminating every dream.

The Invisible Threads of Time

Weaving tales in shadowed hours,
Invisible threads that intertwine,
Capturing moments, fleeting flowers,
In the fabric of design.

Each strand a story, soft and light,
Pulling hearts to where we've been,
Binding souls in dim twilight,
Where the past is never seen.

Echoes linger, whispers fade,
Marking paths we choose to tread,
Through the dreams and plans we laid,
In the silence, secrets spread.

Time will bend, yet still we chase,
Shadows of what used to be,
In the weave, we find our place,
Threads of fate, forever free.

Requiem for the Unremembered

In quiet graves, the lost reside,
Silent whispers, tales unseen,
Memories fade, like the tide,
In shadows, where they've been.

The world moves on, yet they remain,
Ghostly echoes of the past,
Traces of joy mixed with pain,
Marking lives that couldn't last.

Each heartbeat once a vibrant song,
Now a specter, barely known,
Their stories hidden, yet so strong,
In the silence, seeds are sown.

We gather here, with heavy hearts,
To honor souls who flew away,
A requiem as time departs,
In memory, they forever stay.

The Soft Glow of Hidden Truths

Beneath the layers, shadows play,
Softly glowing, truths await,
In the silence, echoes sway,
Revealing paths that lead to fate.

The heart knows where to seek and find,
Whispers hidden from the light,
Guided by the tender mind,
In the dark, they shine so bright.

With gentle hands, we lift the veil,
Unravel threads of fears and dreams,
In the soft glow, we shall sail,
Finding strength in quiet streams.

Truth, a garden yet to bloom,
Nestled deep within the soul,
In the shadows, no more gloom,
Illuminated, we feel whole.

Unraveled Threads of Silence

In whispers soft, the shadows creep,
The echoes linger, secrets keep.
Through muted halls, where silence sighs,
Forgotten dreams in quiet lies.

Once vibrant tales have become faint,
A tapestry that time did taint.
Each thread unspooled, a story lost,
In the stillness, we count the cost.

With every step, the past draws near,
In delicate shadows, ghosts appear.
They sigh and beckon, calling me,
To unearth what is meant to be.

Yet in the quiet, I must tread,
For silence sings where hearts have bled.
What's left behind, I cannot hold,
In unraveled threads, the truth unfolds.

Faint Traces of What Once Was

Upon the ground, where shadows dance,
Lie remnants of a fleeting chance.
Faint traces whisper, soft and low,
Of laughter long since turned to woe.

In corners where the memories dwell,
Time's embrace casts a gentle spell.
Each faded mark, each quiet sigh,
Holds stories of the days gone by.

The echoes of a brighter dawn,
In hallowed halls where joy was drawn.
Yet now they linger, dim and faint,
Like melodies of a calming saint.

As footsteps fade on gravel paths,
I ponder all that time surpasses.
In these traces of what was lost,
I seek the dreams that pay the cost.

Beneath the Layers of Time

Beneath the earth, the secrets hide,
In silent depths, where thoughts abide.
Layers thick with dust and stone,
Stories woven, now overthrown.

Year upon year, the world will change,
Yet buried truths may still arrange.
In every crack, in every fold,
Lies life's essence, brave and bold.

Patterns shifting, shadows play,
Unraveling the dusk of day.
We dig and strive to bring to light,
The buried dreams that ignite our plight.

So here we stand, with hands of hope,
Through time's embrace, we learn to cope.
In layers deep, the past shall find,
A way to echo through the mind.

The Unwritten Chronicles

In fragile ink, the world awaits,
Unwritten tales by fate's own gates.
Each heart a book, yet to be read,
Dreams linger softly, words unsaid.

Across the pages, we all yearn,
For stories held, for lessons learned.
What path we choose, we cannot see,
In written fate, we long to be.

Moments fleeting, like grains of sand,
Each choice we make, a guiding hand.
In the silence, the stories rise,
The unwritten calls, through faithful ties.

So pen your truth, let visions flow,
In unwritten chronicles, we grow.
For in the space where silence dwells,
The story waits, and magic swells.

Faded Footprints in the Dust

Once we walked this path together,
Laughter echoed in the breeze.
Now I trace each step alone,
Lost in memories like fallen leaves.

The sun begins to set once more,
Casting shadows where we stood.
Each print a whisper of the past,
Fleeting moments misunderstood.

Time erases what was dear,
Yet still, I wander through the years.
Searching for a trace of you,
In the silence, I fight my fears.

Softly sighs the evening air,
As stars emerge, one by one.
I hold on to these faded prints,
Remembering when we were young.

Lighthouses of Yesterday's Light

In distant shores where dreams collide,
Stood lighthouses of yesteryears.
Their beams of hope, a guiding force,
Through tempests fierce and unspoken fears.

Crimson skies and salt-kissed winds,
Tales of mariners long gone by.
Each beacon shines with whispered truths,
A promise made beneath the sky.

Though time has worn their sturdy stone,
Their spirits linger, bright and bold.
With every wave that crashes down,
New stories rise, once more retold.

We sail the seas of memory,
Through storms that shape our endless nights.
With every pulse of distant lights,
We navigate to find our rights.

The Cracked Mirror of Reflection

In the shards of a broken glass,
Images flicker, dance, and fade.
Faces lost in time's embrace,
Tell stories of dreams we made.

Each crack a line, a tale unwound,
Where joy and sorrow blend as one.
The past reflects in scattered light,
In memories, our battles won.

I gaze upon the fractured view,
Seeking pieces of who I was.
Through fragile fragments, truth appears,
In every flaw, an honest buzz.

Yet underneath the surface lies,
A strength that time cannot erase.
In every crack, a lesson learned,
In every break, a chance for grace.

Half-Remembered Secrets

Whispers linger in the night,
Secrets hidden, soft as air.
Fleeting glimpses of a world,
Where innocence was laid bare.

In the corners of the mind,
Fragments argue, clash, and play.
What was once a clear design,
Now fades softly into gray.

I remember laughter's sound,
The thrill of stories shared so wide.
In the haze of time, they blur,
Leaving me to question pride.

Yet within these half-formed words,
A magic waits, unspoken still.
To unravel what binds us close,
In essence, find our common will.

Lost Among the Fragments

In shadows deep where whispers dwell,
Fragments of dreams, a silent bell.
Scattered pieces of what once was,
Echoes linger, without a cause.

A heart still seeks the missing part,
In every corner, a hidden art.
Lost in time, the paths we tread,
Footsteps fading, the words unsaid.

Through the shards, a story gleams,
Each fragment holds forgotten dreams.
In twilight's grasp, we try to find,
The scattered pieces of the mind.

Yet in the dark, there's hope to cling,
A melody of what we bring.
Though lost, we gain a deeper view,
Among the fragments, we start anew.

The Forgotten Flavors of Life

Beneath the surface, tastes once bold,
Savoring moments, memories told.
Sweetness lingers in the air,
Life's simple joys, beyond compare.

Colors fade, yet some remain,
In every bite, a hint of pain.
The spice of laughter, the salt of tears,
Seasoning our days throughout the years.

A banquet of dreams, we once enjoyed,
With flavors rich, never destroyed.
Yet time can dull a vibrant tune,
Chasing echoes beneath the moon.

Let us gather, share the feast,
Rekindle love, and find our peace.
In the kitchen of our heart's delight,
We rediscover lost flavors bright.

Traces of an Obscured Light

In realms where shadows gently play,
Traces linger, guide the way.
A flicker lost in twilight's veil,
Yet whispers echo, soft and frail.

In silence deep, the spark resides,
A broken path where hope abides.
Through cracks of doubt, we glimpse the glow,
A warmth that struggles to bestow.

Though clouds may cloak the sky so wide,
The light insists, it will not hide.
Each ray a promise, bold and bright,
Emerging slowly, day by night.

So follow closely, heed the signs,
In every heart, a light that shines.
Obscured it may be, but still it glows,
A beacon bright, where courage grows.

The Quiet Beneath the Roar

Amidst the chaos, a hush doth lie,
Beneath the roar, a whispered sigh.
In every heartbeat, stillness reigns,
A tranquil pulse, where peace remains.

The storm might rage, the waves might crash,
Yet deep within, there lies a stash.
A calmness hidden, soft and slow,
A secret stream, a gentle flow.

In every battle, a silent prayer,
Hope emerges from bleak despair.
The quiet strength found within each soul,
A grounding force that makes us whole.

So listen close, in times of strife,
To the quiet that cradles life.
For in the silence, wisdom blooms,
A vibrant dance amid the dooms.

The Disappearing Reverie

In dreams we danced, silent and free,
Whispers of joy in twilight's plea.
Moments fading like the dusk,
Leaving behind a soft, sweetusk.

The stars blink down with secret smiles,
Carving our path through starlit miles.
Memories drift like leaves in flight,
As dawn approaches, dimming night.

We chase the echoes of yesterday,
While sunlight steals our dreams away.
Yet in our hearts, they softly glow,
A reverie where love can flow.

Hold me close as the night departs,
And weave our dreams in tender hearts.
For in the stillness, we find our grace,
In the disappearing time and space.

Chasing Shadows Through the Mist

Through the fog, we wander lost,
Seeking magic, no matter the cost.
Shadows flicker like whispers of old,
Stories forgotten, waiting to be told.

Each step unfolds a tale anew,
In the embrace of the smoky hue.
Chasing echoes of laughter and light,
Through the haze of the deepening night.

The world grows dim, yet hearts ablaze,
We chase the shadows through a misty maze.
Every corner hides a secret so dear,
In the silent moments, our dreams appear.

So here we linger, beyond the dawn,
Holding tight to the spark we've drawn.
For in the chase, we truly find,
The beauty that lies in love entwined.

Whispers of Distant Shadows

In the quiet, whispers drift,
Carried softly, a gentle gift.
Distant shadows dance and weave,
Secrets hidden, but we believe.

Voices echo through the trees,
Swaying lightly in the breeze.
Mysteries linger on the air,
As night unfolds its silken care.

The moonlight paints the world in dreams,
Flowing softly like silver streams.
Lost in wonder, together we roam,
Finding solace, a place called home.

In the distance, shadows call,
Every heartbeat, a gentle thrall.
Together we chase what lies ahead,
In the whispers of the night, we tread.

Echoes Beneath the Surface

Beneath the waves, a world unfolds,
Whispered stories, ancient and bold.
Echoes linger, soft and clear,
Carried gently through the years.

The surface shimmers with secrets untold,
While currents dance in the grip of the cold.
In the depths, life thrums with grace,
Hidden wonders in a sacred space.

We dive deep, hearts aligned,
Emerging with treasures entwined.
Every ripple breeds a new refrain,
In the echoes that whisper our names.

Hold your breath as we journey down,
Through the shadows where dreams abound.
For beneath the surface, we're forever bound,
In the echoes of love, a treasure found.

Tapestry of Obscured Truths

Threads of shadows intertwine,
Beneath the fabric of the night.
Whispers of secrets left behind,
Color the darkness, dim the light.

Stories hidden, veils in place,
Unraveled tales in fractured time.
Each stitch holds a forgotten face,
A narrative in muted rhyme.

What lurks beneath the woven shroud?
A tapestry of dreams and fears.
In silence, thoughts begin to crowd,
Lost in the echoes of the years.

Illuminate what lies within,
These tangled threads, a truth obscured.
With every pull, the past grows thin,
Yet in the depths, our hope's ensured.

Sunlight on Forgotten Whispers

The morning breaks with gentle grace,
Sunshine spills on dusty lore.
Whispers float in warm embrace,
Calling back the tales of yore.

Memories dance in golden rays,
Lifting voices long since hushed.
In the light, the heart obeys,
Smiles awaken, dreams are brushed.

Time wraps round like a tender vine,
Binding past to present's glow.
What was lost can still align,
As sunlight tames the ebb and flow.

A fleeting moment, lost but found,
In brightness, secrets share their tune.
Forgotten whispers wrap around,
As daylight sings a soft cocoon.

The Echo Chamber of Silence

In corridors where shadows creep,
Thoughts are echoes, loud yet faint.
The weight of stillness in deep sweep,
A chamber built for lips that paint.

Words unspoken cling to the walls,
Resonating in the quiet air.
Each secret held, the heart enthralls,
A solitude that few may bear.

Reverberations of what was said,
Bounce 'gainst thoughts that dare to roam.
Within this space, the mind is fed,
A prison built, devoid of home.

Yet outside lies the world so vast,
Abundant with the voice of fate.
In silence, we hold shadows cast,
While echoes twist and reverberate.

Lost Gleams in Twilight

As dusk falls gently on the scene,
Fading light hints at the day.
Twilight glimmers, soft and keen,
Where dreams in colors begin to sway.

Beneath the sky's fragile embrace,
Stars awaken in the night.
Lost gleams dance in every space,
Welcoming whispers, serene light.

Shadows stretch, embracing grace,
Tales unfold in whispered sighs.
In this realm where time leaves trace,
One can find the truth that lies.

In twilight's calm, let worries cease,
As moments weave into the dark.
Lost in gleams, our minds find peace,
In the night, igniting a spark.

Embracing the Shadows of the Past

In the dim light of fading dreams,
Memories whisper, tug at seams.
Ghosts of laughter, echoes of cries,
In silence, the heart both longs and sighs.

Dusty paths where shadows roam,
Every step leads me back home.
Fragments of joy, shards of pain,
In the shadows, I find my gain.

Reflections dance in twilight's glow,
Lessons learned, seeds to sow.
Embracing grief, and love so vast,
Finding strength in the shadows cast.

With open arms, I hold my fears,
Transforming whispers into cheers.
In every shadow, there's a light,
Guiding me through the endless night.

Labyrinths of Lurking Thoughts

Winding paths of endless schemes,
A mind adrift in tangled dreams.
Each corner turned reveals a choice,
Lost in silence; no guiding voice.

Echoes linger, questions collide,
Within the maze, doubts reside.
Chasing shadows that slip away,
In labyrinths where phantoms play.

Fleeting visions, moments sprawl,
Glimmers of truth begin to call.
Creeping fears whisper to stay,
Yet the heart leads a different way.

Navigating through the maze,
Facing thoughts, through shadows I gaze.
In the chaos, clarity shines,
Finding peace within the lines.

Glances into the Abyss of Time

Time flows like a river wide,
Waves of change cannot be denied.
With every glance, a story unfolds,
Tales of warmth and echoes of bold.

Moments cherished, moments lost,
In the abyss, I count the cost.
Fragments of life in swirling tides,
History's burdens, where pain resides.

Yet in the depths, hope flickers bright,
Guiding us through the endless night.
In every sorrow, lessons embrace,
In the abyss, we find our place.

As clocks tick on, we seek to find,
A balance of heart and restless mind.
Glances held with reverence and grace,
In the flow of time, we find our space.

The Last Notes of Distant Melodies

Soft whispers float on the breeze,
Carried far, through ancient trees.
Fading echoes of songs once sung,
The heart remembers, forever young.

Each note a journey, a tale to share,
In the melody, love lingers there.
A symphony of joy and strife,
Resonating the pulse of life.

Gentle chords that rise and fall,
In the silence, I hear their call.
Notes that dance on the edge of night,
Painting shadows in the fading light.

As the last refrain fades away,
Leaves a memory, come what may.
In distant echoes, I find my peace,
In the last notes, my soul's release.

Familiar Strangers in the Mist

In shadows where the whispers dwell,
Figures dance like dreams that fell.
Eyes meet knowing, yet not clear,
Familiar faces drawn so near.

Through the fog, we trace our steps,
Past memories, where silence wept.
Each breath caught in fleeting light,
We wander lost in shared twilight.

Their laughter echoes, sweet yet strange,
Within the mist, we all exchange.
Stories carved in softest air,
Layers of life, woven with care.

As dawn breaks through the hazy veil,
These strangers roam, yet hearts prevail.
Though paths diverge in time's own game,
Our souls remember, still the same.

Pale Echoes of a Forgotten Sound

In a hollow hall where ghosts reside,
Whispers linger, like the tide.
Each note forgotten, a soft refrain,
Chasing shadows, boundless pain.

Faint melodies of days gone by,
Drift through corners where silence sighs.
In the stillness, the heart recalls,
Echoes trapped within the walls.

Voices weave through the fragile air,
A symphony of what was rare.
Notes like dreams begin to fade,
Lost in a dance, the past displayed.

Yet in the silence, hope resides,
In memories where time confides.
Though sounds may fade, their essence lives,
In each heartbeat, the past still gives.

The Space Where Stories Linger

Beneath the oak, where shadows play,
Tales entwine in light and gray.
A tapestry of lives unfolds,
In whispered winds, our truth retold.

Each wrinkle carved in ancient bark,
Holds secrets of the light and dark.
In every sigh, a life once known,
The space we share, forever sown.

Time dances lightly on these stones,
Weaving dreams with fragile tones.
Here, the past and future meet,
In quiet grace, our hearts repeat.

So gather close, let stories breeze,
In every moment, memories tease.
For in this space where echoes blend,
Our souls connect, our journeys mend.

Faint Heartbeats in Stolen Time

In stolen glances, moments meet,
Faint heartbeats quicken, soft and sweet.
Ticking clocks can't claim our fire,
In secret spaces, we conspire.

The world outside begins to fade,
In shadows where our dreams are laid.
With every whispered, longing sigh,
We trace the stars that paint the sky.

Time stretches wide as we let go,
In this stillness, feelings grow.
Each heartbeat echoes, tender, bright,
A dance of souls in quiet light.

As twilight falls, we linger on,
In stolen hours, our hearts are drawn.
Though time may chase, we'll hold it tight,
In these faint heartbeats, we find our light.

Between the Pages of Absence

In whispered words that fade away,
A silence hums, it tries to stay.
Once filled with laughter, now just sighs,
A tale of love where sorrow lies.

The corners age, the edges fray,
Each page turned brings time's decay.
Yet still I seek in shadows cast,
Those moments bright that couldn't last.

I trace the lines, the ink worn thin,
Remnants of warmth where we begin.
Each heartbeat echoes in the void,
Between the pages, love destroyed.

Ephemeral Hues of Memory

A fleeting blush of sunset's glow,
Paints dreamy skies, a vibrant show.
Each moment gilded, soon to fade,
An artwork crafted, time betrayed.

The laughter lingers like perfume,
In gentle shades, a heart's costume.
Yet shadows creep as daylight fades,
In twilight's grasp, the promise wades.

Remembered smiles, like petals fall,
An echo's dance, a silken call.
Traces of joy, like whispers spin,
In these rich hues, we live within.

Fractured Pieces of Time

Shattered moments on the floor,
Glass reflections of what was before.
Each shard a story, sharp and bright,
Fragments lost in endless night.

With every breath, the pieces clash,
Remnants linger, shadows flash.
Time, a puzzle, hard to mend,
Where beginnings and endings blend.

Yet in the chaos, beauty lies,
A mosaic formed beneath the skies.
Each fractured piece, a glimpse divine,
In the canvas of lost time.

The Unseen Gallery of Dreams

In silence hangs the dreamer's art,
Unseen portraits of every heart.
Brush strokes dance on air unseen,
In every wish, a quiet sheen.

Imagination's whispers call,
To hidden galleries, vast and tall.
Each dream a canvas, vast and wide,
In colors bold, where secrets hide.

Reality blurs, the veil is thin,
In this enchantment, we all spin.
A gallery where hopes collide,
In unseen worlds, our hearts reside.

Rusted Keys of Old Dreams

Once locked away in a chest,
Faded memories linger still.
The keys whisper of lost quests,
Echoes of a gentle thrill.

Each turn unlocks a new dawn,
Secrets woven in rusted gold.
What was lost now feels reborn,
With stories from ages old.

Fingers trace away the dust,
In the corners where shadows creep.
Every key reveals its trust,
Beneath the watchful moon's peep.

In dreams where time intertwines,
Fragments of hope softly gleam.
Rusted keys, old as the pines,
Open doors to a vibrant dream.

The Timelessness of Lost Glimpses

Moments dance in twilight's haze,
Fleeting glances linger near.
Through the mist, a foggy gaze,
Holds a season made of fear.

In the alleys where shadows play,
Echoes of laughter softly wane.
With each memory on display,
Time unravels, yet remains.

Whispers of an ancient song,
Crossing paths we never chose.
In this timeline, we belong,
Walking where the river flows.

Yet in dreams, the past ignites,
Lost glimpses shimmer like the stars.
Timeless tales in starry nights,
Trace the journey of our scars.

Resonating Silence of Untold Tales

In the stillness, stories sleep,
Hidden deep within the dark.
Each silence, a promise to keep,
Where echoes dance and softly spark.

Voices trapped in whispered words,
Waiting for the chance to soar.
Among the leaves, where hope is stirred,
Untold tales weave evermore.

A canvas painted, void of sound,
Yet colors rise in vivid dreams.
Within the quiet, they are found,
Flowing like uncharted streams.

Resonating through the night,
Secrets waiting for their time.
In silence, they take flight,
A symphony of endless rhyme.

The Language of Unfinished Journeys

Footsteps linger on the path,
Echoes of journeys yet to start.
With every end, a silent laugh,
Guiding us to play our part.

Maps unrolled on barren lands,
Lines that twist in faded ink.
A language spoken with our hands,
Invites us deeper, dare we think.

Destinations lie ahead,
Yet here we sigh and dream awake.
In the spaces we once tread,
Awaits the love we dared to stake.

Unfinished, still we move along,
Writing verses in the sand.
Every heartbeat is a song,
In the language of the land.

Whispers of Dust

In the corners where silence dwells,
Fleeting memories weave their spells.
Sunlight dances on golden beams,
Time flickers like forgotten dreams.

Fragments of laughter cling to air,
Soft echoes linger everywhere.
Footsteps trace where shadows play,
Whispers of dust from yesterday.

Chasing moments cloaked in haze,
Faint silhouettes of brighter days.
Each sigh a story left unsaid,
In the twilight, secrets spread.

A tapestry of all that's lost,
The warmth of love, the chilling frost.
Yet in the hush, we find our peace,
In whispers of dust, our souls will cease.

Echoes of Yesterday

Beneath the veil of twilight's grace,
Memories linger, time can't erase.
The laughter of friends long gone,
Calls me back to where I belong.

Cracked photographs, faded and worn,
Each tells a tale, the past reborn.
In every shadow, a familiar face,
Time's tender touch, a warm embrace.

Through rusted gates and twilight's glow,
Whispers of lives that once did flow.
In echoes soft, their voices sing,
Of fleeting joy, and fleeting spring.

Though seasons change and moments flee,
The heart remembers what it can see.
In the echo of yesterday's song,
We find the place where we belong.

Shadows in the Attic

In the attic, where shadows creep,
Silent secrets, buried deep.
Old trunks hold tales of yesteryear,
Ghostly whispers seem to near.

Dust motes dance in fading light,
Relics of dreams take silent flight.
Each crack and crevice, a story waits,
In the stillness, time dictates.

Forgotten toys and letters stained,
Whispers of love, both lost and gained.
In cobwebbed corners, echoes sigh,
Where laughter lived, now shadows lie.

Yet in this gloom, a flicker glows,
The warmth of memories still flows.
In shadows deep, we find our way,
To touch the past, to live today.

The Haunt of Hidden Dreams

In the depths of silent night,
Dreams awaken, take to flight.
Veiled in whispers, soft and bright,
They dance like stars, igniting light.

Beneath the surface, thoughts entwine,
In the maze of heart and mind,
Hidden wishes, often rare,
In the quiet, they declare.

Shadows linger, doubts may rise,
Yet every dream has a disguise.
In the dark, they weave their threads,
The haunt of dreams, where courage treads.

Among the stars, a promise gleams,
A gentle nudge, the push of dreams.
In this space, we dare to chase,
The visions waiting to embrace.

The Ghosts of Abandoned Paths

Whispers haunt the overgrown trails,
Where shadows linger, and time derails.
Footsteps lost, in the leaves they fade,
A tapestry of memories laid.

Broken chains and rusted gates,
Tell stories of love and bitter fates.
Nature reclaims what once was known,
In silence, the past finds its throne.

Moonlight dances on crumbled stone,
Echoes of laughter, now overgrown.
Every turn holds a tale to tell,
Of wanderers who dared to dwell.

Yet in the stillness, hope persists,
For paths may widen, and dreams exist.
With each step, the heartbeats guide,
Through the ghosts where memories reside.

Sifting Through the Ashes

Embers flicker in the morning light,
Fragments of dreams fade out of sight.
Once a fire, now warm despair,
Loss lingers softly, fills the air.

Hands sift through remains, with care,
Cherished moments lost, laid bare.
Memories crackle, smoke and swirl,
In the chaos, life's stories unfurl.

From charred ruins, new seeds must sprout,
A testament to love, without doubt.
Through sorrow's veil, hope breaks anew,
For from ashes, we rise and pursue.

Whispers of past intertwine with grace,
In every heart, there's a sacred space.
Time moves slowly, yet still we strive,
To build from the remnants, and truly thrive.

Unraveled Threads of Memory

A tapestry woven, yet frayed at the seams,
Threads of the past dance in waking dreams.
Moments stitched close, then pulled apart,
Each strand a whisper, a piece of the heart.

Colors fade softly, but stories remain,
In the fabric of life, joy, and pain.
As needles entwine, old tales unfold,
In the warmth of the memories, forever bold.

Remembered laughter in a tangled skein,
Hopes intertwined, like lovers in rain.
Though distance may pull, and time rearrange,
The essence of us will never change.

So gather the threads, and weave anew,
For in every ending, begins something true.
Life's quilt is stitched with a tender hand,
Unraveled threads, together, we stand.

Chasing Fleeting Echoes

Footsteps tread softly on the breeze,
Chasing whispers that tease the trees.
Echoes of laughter, a distant chime,
Fleeting moments, suspended in time.

Across the meadows, shadows play,
Dancing with dusk at the end of the day.
Every heartbeat a reminder to chase,
The beauty of life, in this sacred space.

Yet shadows retreat, as light starts to fade,
Memories linger, but can't be remade.
In the twilight, secrets slip away,
Leaving traces of dreams that chose to stay.

So run with the echoes, embrace the flight,
For life is a whisper, a flickering light.
Let the moments unfurl, wild and free,
In the dance of existence, find harmony.

Lingering Notes from the Past

Whispers in shadow, soft and low,
Memories dance where time won't go.
Faded laughter echoes wide,
In the heart where dreams still bide.

Fingers trace the worn-out page,
Every line, a golden sage.
Moments trapped, like dew on grass,
In the stillness, memories pass.

The clock ticks softly, a gentle chime,
Holding stories within its rhyme.
Old melodies linger, sweet and clear,
As the past leans in to hear.

Through windows cracked, the sunlight streams,
Illuminating forgotten dreams.
In every echo, a truth unfolds,
In lingering notes, the past still holds.

The Silent Music of Forgotten Years

Silent songs of days gone by,
Drift like clouds in a tranquil sky.
Each note a brush of soft refrain,
A serenade of joy and pain.

Shadows dance on faded walls,
While the memory softly calls.
In the silence, a heartbeat lies,
Wrapped in whispers, the past complies.

Footsteps trace the path of time,
Rhythms lost, yet still they climb.
Through the ages, echoes gleam,
In forgotten notes, we seek the dream.

The harmony of days unspun,
Plays on, though the years are done.
In quietude, our hearts conjoin,
To the silent music we still join.

Mosaics of Lost Visions

Fragments scattered, colors bright,
Shattered dreams in the pale moonlight.
Each piece a story, each crack a sigh,
In the heart's gallery, they lie.

Shards of longing, hopes entwined,
Captured moments in stillness confined.
Beneath the surface, truths remain,
In the mosaic of joy and pain.

Each tile a whisper, a tale to tell,
Of love once kindled, of times that fell.
In the chaos, a portrait grows,
Of lost visions, as the spirit flows.

Life's tapestry, woven dear,
Holds all the laughter, captures the fear.
In every flaw, a beauty sings,
In mosaics of past, the heart still clings.

Beneath the Weight of Old Stories

Beneath the weight of tales long spun,
Lie shadows woven, races won.
Threads of history, tightly bound,
In every word, the past is found.

A tapestry rich, of joy and strife,
Each stitch a moment of a life.
Through every sorrow, every cheer,
Old stories whisper, always near.

In twilight moments, the echoes call,
Inviting hearts to rise, to fall.
Underneath the burdened night,
Old stories cradle, holding tight.

Here we gather, hearts laid bare,
To share the burdens that all must bear.
In the telling, we find release,
Beneath the weight, we share our peace.

Sighs in the Space Between

Whispers drift on silence's breath,
In shadows where time bows to rest.
Fleeting moments held too tight,
A dance in the corners of night.

Soft echoes whisper through the air,
Yearning hearts feel the gentle stare.
In the hush, a promise glows,
In the space, where love still flows.

Dusty Portraits of Yesteryears

Frames lined with shadows and dust,
Faded memories wrapped in rust.
Each glance reveals a cherished face,
Stories lost in time and space.

Colors bleed and slowly fade,
Moments linger like a serenade.
The past, a ghost that softly treads,
In the heart, where the story spreads.

Shadows Cast by Unspoken Words

In the stillness, silence lays,
Words tangled in a quiet haze.
Promises linger, unformed dreams,
Echoes caught in moonlit beams.

Eyes that convey what lips cannot,
Each glance a treasure, a secret thought.
Between the lines of hearts entwined,
A symphony of souls combined.

The Memory Keepers of Through Ages

Guardians of moments, time's embrace,
Holding stories in a sacred space.
With gentle hands, they cradle light,
Illuminating shadows of the night.

Through chapters woven with tender care,
They shape the love that hangs in air.
Each heartbeat, a treasured song,
In memory's arms, we all belong.

Visions in the Margins

In whispers soft, the tales arise,
Between the lines, where silence lies.
Each faded page, a story spun,
Of hidden thoughts, and dreams undone.

Shadows dance on paper thin,
Echoes of where we've been.
The ink reveals what eyes can't see,
A world alive, yet bound to be.

Drawn in margins, secrets kept,
In every corner, silence wept.
The visions speak of what could be,
A fleeting glimpse, a memory.

So turn the leaf and look again,
In the margins, truth remains.
Each scribble holds a heart's refrain,
In whispered tones, forever plain.

Derelict Dreams of Old

Beneath the rust of time-worn frames,
Lie scattered hopes, forgotten names.
In silence thick, the echoes roam,
In derelict halls, they seek a home.

Once vibrant walls now paint decay,
Where laughter lived, has slipped away.
Ghosts of joy in shadowed rooms,
Haunted whispers of past glooms.

A fractured mirror reflects the pain,
Of fading dreams in the rain.
In crumbling bricks, the stories fold,
Of wishful hearts, now grown cold.

Yet among the dust and broken seams,
The heart still fights for those old dreams.
In memory's light, they softly glow,
Through dereliction, love can grow.

The Pathways to Lost Worlds

Beneath the stars, the roads unwind,
To lands forgotten, dreams defined.
Through whispers of the ancient trees,
Lost worlds beckon with the breeze.

A flicker here, a shimmer there,
The veil is thin, the magic rare.
In shadowed trails and starlit glades,
Adventure calls, its voice cascades.

With every step, the stories thrive,
In twilight's glow, the spirits drive.
Through twisted paths and secret doors,
The heart embarks on tales of yore.

So journey forth, embrace the unknown,
In lost worlds, we've never grown.
For time is but a fleeting dream,
In pathways lost, we find our theme.

The Quiet After the Storm

When thunder fades and rain's refrain,
Leaves whispers soft, like gentle rain.
The world holds breath, as peace descends,
In quiet shades, where stillness mends.

Around the bend, the sun will rise,
To paint the sky with tender sighs.
Each droplet falls, a memory kept,
In nature's calm, the heart has leapt.

Branches bow from weight of tears,
Yet in their bend, lies hope, not fears.
For after storms, the blooms return,
In silence deep, their colors burn.

Hold close this calm, in fleeting time,
The quiet whispers, soft as rhyme.
For after dark, the light will bloom,
In valleys sweet, dispelling gloom.

When Memories Drift Away

In the stillness of the night,
Whispers of laughter fade.
Frozen moments take flight,
In the twilight's gentle shade.

Faded photographs in hand,
Colors dimmed, tones of gray.
Echoes from a distant land,
As memories drift away.

Beneath the stars, names are etched,
In the silence, we recall.
Each heartbeat, a lesson fetched,
Through shadows that rise and fall.

Time meanders like a stream,
Carrying dreams far from view.
Yet in silence, still we dream,
For the past will always be true.

The Unwritten Chronicles

Pages blank, a tale untold,
In the corners, stories hide.
Whispers soft, yet bold,
In the quiet, dreams abide.

A feather pen waits in vain,
To ink the thoughts that swirl.
Boundless worlds yet to gain,
In the heart of every girl.

Ink drops fall like gentle rain,
Creating paths where none have been.
Living tales can break the chain,
Of all that lies within.

Dare to write beyond the lines,
Let your spirit's voice be free.
The unwritten, it defines,
Every dream that longs to be.

Shadows of Abandoned Places

Crumbled walls and broken doors,
Silence sings a mournful tune.
Nature weaves through forgotten floors,
Beneath the watchful moon.

Windows frame the ghostly light,
Through the dust, a story sways.
Echoes whisper of the night,
Where dreams were once ablaze.

Footsteps fade on haunted ground,
While the past reaches a hand.
In the stillness, truths are found,
In shadows, we understand.

Time has etched a fading grace,
In places left to decay.
Yet beauty dwells in lost space,
Where memories softly lay.

The Archive of Silent Souls

In a vault of dreams, they rest,
Silent voices, tales untold.
Captured whispers, every quest,
In the folds of time, they hold.

Forgotten names etched in stone,
Beneath the weight of time's embrace.
Longing for the light they've known,
In the quiet, find their place.

Each heartbeat, a melody spun,
In the chamber of the past.
In every soul, a journey run,
Echoes meant to forever last.

Open the archive, let them be,
From shadows, they find their way.
In the stories, hearts run free,
Their spirits dance, come what may.

The Veil of Unseen Stories

Behind the curtain, shadows dance,
Whispers echo, lost in chance.
Threads of fate, a tapestry spun,
Silent tales of battles won.

In the stillness, secrets breathe,
Hushed confessions, weaves sheathe.
Ink of time stains the page,
Histories wrapped in quiet rage.

Memories linger in cool night air,
Fleeting glimpses, we must beware.
Fragments shimmer in the dark,
Illuminating the hidden spark.

Each heartbeat holds a story true,
Waiting for lips to break the blue.
Unseen paths that softly call,
In this veil, we find our all.

Remnants of Yesterday's Dreams

Whispers of hope in the morning light,
Fable whispers, dreams take flight.
Echoes linger on the breeze,
Fragments lost like autumn leaves.

Time drapes nostalgia like a cloak,
Silent verses that never spoke.
In the corners, visions hide,
Hopes once cherished, cast aside.

A treasure trove of what was dear,
Carved in hearts, inscribed in fear.
Yet from the shadows, they arise,
Awakening sparkles in our eyes.

The past may fade, but won't depart,
Each remnant resonates the heart.
In fleeting moments, dreams still gleam,
A dance of yesterday's daring dream.

Silhouettes in Faded Light

Figures move in twilight's haze,
Cast upon the evening's gaze.
Softly merged with dusk's embrace,
Shapes like memories we can trace.

Whispers linger, shadows blend,
Faded outlines, time we spend.
In the stillness, echoes play,
Lost reflections of yesterday.

Flickering candles, moments shared,
In hushed tones, our hearts declared.
A canvas drawn with muted strokes,
In quiet whispers, love awoke.

As stars emerge in velvet skies,
We find ourselves in silent sighs.
In silhouettes, our truths ignite,
Bound in the warmth of faded light.

Secrets Woven in Dust

In corners, secrets sit and wait,
Stories etched by chance and fate.
Dusty shelves with tales concealed,
Hearts of longing, unsealed.

Memories whisper, ancient threads,
Laughter mingles with words unsaid.
Each grain holds a life once lived,
Echoes found in what we give.

Through the window, daylight streams,
Revealing all our hidden dreams.
Whispered stories on the breeze,
Gentle chimes in rustling leaves.

As we sift through time's embrace,
We find our truth in every trace.
In dust, the past unfurls its wings,
Secrets woven in whispered things.

Entwined in the Forgotten

Whispers echo through the trees,
Where shadows dance and time will freeze.
Lost moments cling like fading mist,
In memories' arms, we still persist.

Fingers trace the paths once known,
On old, worn pages, wisdom's sown.
Laughter mingles with the sighs,
In every glance, a love that lies.

We build again what fate has torn,
In threads of gold, a bond reborn.
Through tangled roots, our hearts entwine,
In silent vows, forever thine.

Among the ruins, hopes still bloom,
In secret corners, dispel the gloom.
For in the depths of what we've lost,
Rises anew, though love is tossed.

Glimmers in the Dusty Attic

In corners packed with memories old,
Dust motes dance like stories told.
Boxes hold treasures wrapped in time,
Fragments of laughter, shadows in rhyme.

Forgotten toys and faded dreams,
Whispers of laughter in silent screams.
Faded photographs, smiles that shine,
Each glimmer a tale, a life's design.

An old piano with keys that sigh,
Hums forgotten tunes that softly lie.
Notes drift like wisps of love long gone,
In the dim light, hearts linger on.

The attic breathes with fragrant air,
Each memory woven with tender care.
In dusty realms, we find our way,
Into the echoes of yesterday.

The Space Between Silence and Sound

In the hush before a soft reply,
Moments stretch, as if to pry.
Gazes meet in unspoken fears,
Time holds its breath, as silence nears.

A heartbeat thuds, a whisper calls,
In the quiet, truth enthralls.
Words dance lightly, waiting to break,
In delicate threads, the feelings wake.

Tension hangs like a heavy quilt,
In this void, emotions built.
Tangible hopes flicker, then flick,
In the balance, the magic we pick.

Between the notes, we find our way,
In the silence, we dare to sway.
For in the pause, love's essence found,
In the space between silence and sound.

Beyond the Shades of Memory

In twilight hues, old ghosts appear,
Fragments of laughter, whispers we hear.
Each shadow holds a story untold,
In colors vivid, the past unfolds.

Footsteps echo on paths long gone,
Through corridors where light has shone.
Flickers of joy, tinged with pain,
In every heartbeat, love remains.

We wander the realms of distant dreams,
Through veils of time, the heart redeems.
Scenes replay in a gentle haze,
In every moment, an echo stays.

Beyond the shades, we chase the light,
In twilight's arms, we take our flight.
For in the depths of what we've known,
Lies the warmth of love, forever grown.

Lurking Beneath the Surface

Shadows creep where light won't tread,
Whispers of secrets, softly spread.
In stillness, darkness weaves its thread,
A world concealed, where fears are bred.

Beneath the calm, the currents pull,
A silent breath, a thunder's lull.
Ripples dance, intentions full,
In unseen depths, hearts start to mull.

Voices hide in the soothing night,
Haunting dreams, taking flight.
Echoes call in muted fright,
The surface shimmers, deceiving light.

What lies beneath, we dare not see,
In the quiet spaces, truths decree.
The whispered tales, the mystery,
Lurking deep, forever free.

Forgotten Echoes of Time

Old stones gather dust and decay,
Once vibrant lives, now drift away.
Echoes of laughter, memories sway,
In the shadows, they silently play.

Faded photographs, edges worn,
Capturing moments, tales reborn.
In whispered winds, the past is torn,
Forgotten songs, forever mourn.

Time turns pages, yet some remain,
In quiet corners, love and pain.
The ghosts of history, a gentle chain,
Binding hearts in a timeless strain.

Listen close, the stories breathe,
In silence, lives twist and wreathe.
Forgotten echoes, they bequeath,
The essence of dreams, like autumn's sheath.

Remnants of a Faded Glamour

Once adorned in silk and lace,
Beauty danced with elegant grace.
Now it lingers, a hollow space,
Shadows clutch a bygone place.

Glistening jewels, now dusted gray,
Whispers of dances that led astray.
In the mirror, a ghostly display,
Faded glamour, tucked away.

The grand chandeliers flicker dim,
Echoes of laughter, a fading hymn.
In dim-lit corners, the world grows grim,
Memories cling, precious but slim.

Yet beauty's spirit still remains,
In each fragment, joy and pains.
Past elegance quietly reigns,
With time's passage, the heart retains.

The Silent Histories We Hold

In every heart, a tale untold,
Silent histories in shadows bold.
Echoes of dreams that time won't fold,
Woven in fabric, emotions scrolled.

Between the lines of whispered lore,
Unseen battles, an ancient score.
Each quiet moment, a hidden door,
To lives well-lived, forevermore.

Beneath our skin, the stories gleam,
An endless tapestry, a living stream.
In silence shared, we find the theme,
Of yesterday's love and tomorrow's dream.

Hold close these truths, for they are ours,
In the stillness, time devours.
The silent histories, like blooming flowers,
Awaken hearts and dissolve the towers.

Veils of Unseen Memories

In dusty attic corners, we find
Whispers wrapped in fabric of time.
Each thread a story, woven tight,
Beneath the weight of old sunlight.

Faded photographs and dreams long past,
Echoes of laughter, shadows cast.
A tapestry of moments intertwined,
Veils of the heart, secrets confined.

Time dances softly, a waltz in gray,
Memories flicker, then drift away.
Yet, in the silence, they remain,
Whispering truths, both joy and pain.

Unraveled tales in the quiet night,
Faded ribbons caught in flight.
We hold them close, though they may fade,
Veils of unseen memories, serenade.

When Silence Speaks

In the stillness, secrets bloom,
A language found in quiet gloom.
Words unspoken, yet so profound,
In silence, wisdom can be found.

The pause between each breath we take,
A moment held for truth's own sake.
Melodies of peace whisper low,
When silence speaks, we come to know.

Eyes that meet in knowing grace,
Silent conversations, time and space.
In the gaps where voices cease,
Silence wraps our hearts in peace.

Listen closely, hear the call,
In hushed tones, we can have it all.
Each heartbeat, a soft, gentle plea,
When silence speaks, we're truly free.

Glistening in the Gloom

Moonlight dances on dewy leaves,
Whispers of twilight quietly weaves.
Stars emerge from dusk's embrace,
Glistening softly, a celestial trace.

The world fades in shades of blue,
Secrets hidden in the night's view.
A silver glow on the silent streams,
Glistening in the echoes of dreams.

Shadows stretch, reaching long,
Nature sings a twilight song.
In the stillness, magic looms,
Glistening gently in the glooms.

Hope shines bright in the darkest hour,
Through veils of night, we feel its power.
In every glimmer, life begins,
Glistening softly, where wonder spins.

The Secret Lives of Shadows

In corners where the light won't tread,
Shadows dance, where whispers led.
Silent watchers, they glide and weave,
The secret lives, we dare believe.

Flickering forms in candle's glow,
Tales of the past that ebb and flow.
They guard the thoughts we dare not show,
The secret lives, the currents flow.

Underneath the moon's soft gaze,
Shadows twirl in midnight's maze.
In their depths, illusions blend,
The secret lives, they twist and bend.

From dusk till dawn, they weave their thread,
A tapestry of dreams unsaid.
In every flicker, a story lies,
The secret lives of shadows, wise.

Traces of the Unwritten

In the silence, whispers dwell,
Stories waiting to be fell.
Pages blank, yet filled with dreams,
Lost in shadows, or so it seems.

Footsteps linger on the path,
Guiding hearts through aftermath.
Unraveled tales, they gently weave,
Promises in the air, they breathe.

The ink dries slow, but hope remains,
In the echoes, love sustains.
Every heartbeat, every breath,
Marks the life beyond the death.

In this realm where thoughts are free,
Unwritten words dance silently.
The future calls, a quiet muse,
In every choice, the path we choose.

Pieces of a Distant Echo

In the distance, voices call,
Ghostly shadows, they rise and fall.
Fragments melt like morning mist,
Leaving dreams that can't be missed.

Each note carries a memory,
A melody of history.
Whispers flow like rivers wide,
Beneath the surface, they reside.

Chasing rays of fading light,
Through the corridors of night.
With every heartbeat, they align,
Connecting souls across the line.

In the echoes, fragments gleam,
Pieced together, like a dream.
Through the time, their song will play,
Guiding hearts along the way.

Time's Secret Chamber

Behind the clock, a door is sealed,
Where time's secrets are revealed.
Silent moments, pauses keep,
In hidden chambers, dreams do sleep.

Gently ticking, sands descend,
Whispers in the air transcend.
Every second carries weight,
In this room, we contemplate.

Reflections dance on walls so near,
Memories echo clear and dear.
In the stillness, stories bloom,
Within the dark, there is no gloom.

In time's chamber, we abide,
Every heartbeat, every stride.
Unlock the door, let wonder flow,
In the stillness, feel time grow.

The Quiet Returns of Old Tomorrows

In the dawn of distant dreams,
Quiet whispers drift like streams.
Time moves slow, yet swiftly flows,
In the garden where hope grows.

Old tomorrows paved the way,
Carving paths from night to day.
Their quiet returns softly fall,
Bringing wisdom to us all.

In the heart, we hold these threads,
Memories where the future treads.
Gently rocking, like the tide,
Old tomorrows, our trusted guide.

As shadows fade and bright dawns break,
Embrace the calm that dreams awake.
In the silence, we will find,
The gentle stirrings of the mind.

Hidden Corners of Time

In a quiet nook, shadows play,
Memory whispers where dreams sway.
Dusty tomes hold stories untold,
In hidden corners, mysteries unfold.

Ticking clocks mark the silent hours,
Fading echoes of springtime flowers.
Time weaves secrets through the air,
In hidden corners, we linger there.

Fleeting moments caught in between,
Whispers of life, soft and serene.
The warmth of longing wraps like a shawl,
In hidden corners, we grasp it all.

Beneath the stars, our wishes blend,
In the silence, time seems to suspend.
We find ourselves in the subtle light,
In hidden corners, day turns to night.

The Lament of Lost Moments

Sands slipping through the hourglass tight,
Fleeting seconds fading out of sight.
Each heartbeat whispers tales of regret,
In the lament of lost moments, we fret.

Laughter echoes, now just a sigh,
Wishes made that silently die.
In twilight's glow, shadows fall long,
In the lament of lost moments, we belong.

Photos yellowed, memories blur,
Time moves on, but we still stir.
Stealing glances at what we miss,
In the lament of lost moments, we reminisce.

Yet in the ache, hope softly gleams,
Through the sorrow, a glimmer of dreams.
We seek the light, even when it's gone,
In the lament of lost moments, we press on.

Echoing Voices Through the Gaps

Through the spaces, voices drift,
Carrying tales, a precious gift.
Silent breezes hum forgotten songs,
Echoing voices where time belongs.

Between the lines of whispered thoughts,
The echoes linger, a puzzle sought.
Filling voids with memories bright,
Echoing voices in the fading light.

In the chambers of the heart's deep frame,
Lost in whispers, we call their names.
Each echo dances, a timeless waltz,
Through the gaps where silence exalts.

When night descends, the world grows still,
Echoes of dreams linger on the hill.
In shadows cast, their stories entwine,
Echoing voices, forever divine.

Fragments of a Forgotten Journey

Dusty roads where footprints fade,
Lost in time, the memories laid.
Through tangled paths and brambled thorns,
Fragments of a journey, worn and torn.

Once vibrant tales of laughter shared,
Now faded echoes, no one cared.
In the silence, we search for clues,
Fragments of a journey, we muse.

Letters unsent, wishes laid bare,
The weight of moments we cannot bear.
A suitcase filled with dreams once bright,
Fragments of a journey, lost from sight.

Yet in the midst of faded trails,
Hope still glimmers, love never fails.
We gather pieces, reclaim the past,
Fragments of a journey, hold us fast.

When Time Stands Still

In quiet rooms where shadows play,
The hours stretch, then slip away.
A breath held tight, a whisper low,
In moments vast, our spirits flow.

The ticking clock cannot be heard,
In stillness, dreams find flight, undeterred.
We linger wrapped in twilight's grace,
Time falters in this sacred space.

The world outside begins to fade,
In silence, memories are laid.
On whispered winds, our hearts connect,
When time stands still, we reflect.

Beneath the stars, we float and weave,
In endless night, we dare believe.
Moments lost, yet soft and real,
In frozen time, our souls can heal.

Fragments of an Unspoken Past

In dusty corners, secrets hide,
Echoes of laughter, tears applied.
Pages yellowed, stories untold,
Fragments of life, a treasure of gold.

Voices linger in shadowed halls,
Whispers trapped within the walls.
Each glance exchanged, a heavy cost,
In silent words, so much is lost.

The past a puzzle, pieces stray,
Incomplete, yet here to stay.
In the silence, we search for light,
For truth once spoken, now takes flight.

Each fragment holds a sacred thread,
Binding the living to the dead.
In memories, we seek to find,
The unspoken echoes of our mind.

The Hidden Stories We Bury

In layers deep, we hide our truth,
Stories masked beneath the youth.
Behind closed doors, we wear a guise,
The hidden tales behind our eyes.

With every smile, a shade of grief,
In silent struggles, we seek relief.
In whispered dreams, we tell the tale,
Of hearts that wander, hopes that sail.

The burdens carried, heavy sighs,
In every secret, part of us lies.
Yet strength is found in soft release,
In sharing shadows, there's found peace.

Together, let the stories flow,
For in the light, our spirits grow.
Stories hidden, now we share,
In every heart, love waits somewhere.

Glimpses of Fleeting Whispers

In twilight's hush, a sigh takes flight,
Fleeting whispers in the night.
Glimpses caught on the evening breeze,
Soft secrets shared among the trees.

Moments fleeting, like shadows cast,
In gentle echoes, the die is cast.
We chase the dawn, with hope in hand,
In whispers low, together we stand.

Every heartbeat sings a song,
In fleeting whispers, we belong.
Fragments dance in silver light,
Glimpses whisper of endless night.

In memories stitched, we find our way,
In the quiet, we dare to stay.
Fleeting whispers, tender and bright,
Guide us softly into the night.

Secrets Beneath the Skin

Beneath the layers, shadows dwell,
Whispers hidden, secrets to tell.
Threads of silence, woven tight,
Flickering hopes in the depth of night.

Tales of longing, dreams untold,
Crimson stories, dark and bold.
Each heartbeat pulses with a sigh,
Truths buried deep, where moments lie.

Tender scars show marks of pain,
Silent witnesses of love's refrain.
In every heartbeat, in every tear,
Secrets unfold, yet remain near.

Unravel the fabric, take a peek,
Into the silence where spirits speak.
A dance of shadows, a fleeting trace,
The skin tells stories, time won't erase.

The Unheard Melodies of Memory

Soft echoes linger, whispers of the past,
In corners where shadows whisper fast.
Notes of laughter, lost in the breeze,
Memories flutter like leaves from trees.

Fragments of songs drift through the air,
Carried on whispers, here and there.
In the silence, melodies arise,
Tales of joy hidden from prying eyes.

The heart beats softly with each refrain,
Melodies dance through pleasure and pain.
In forgotten rooms where shadows play,
Dreams weave through the light of day.

Listen closely to the stillness around,
In whispered notes, the lost are found.
Memory's tune is a sacred place,
A melody played at a gentle pace.

Strokes of a Vanished Brush

Faded colors on a canvas bare,
Whispers of beauty, once vibrant and rare.
Strokes of longing left in the dust,
Echoes of passion, in pigments they rust.

Each line tells a tale of heart's desire,
Colors blending in a dance of fire.
Yet time, the thief, has drained the hue,
Where once there was life, now shadows strew.

In the silence, an artist's woe,
Forgotten dreams in a world of pro.
What was once vivid now barely sees,
A glimpse of the heart in a breath of breeze.

Beneath the layers, stories reside,
Of love unspoken and secrets that hide.
Brushes may vanish, but visions remain,
Art speaks softly, beyond the pain.

In the Company of Specters

Echoes linger in the moonlit space,
Whispers of souls, a haunting embrace.
Shadows flicker where memories tread,
Ghosts of the past, where silence is spread.

In twilight's glow, they softly speak,
Tales of what was, of moments unique.
Hand in hand with the shadows that sway,
In the company of specters, we lay.

Time waltzes gently with stories untold,
Carved in the night, like marbled gold.
Each ghostly figure holds a piece of time,
In the dance of remembrance, a silent rhyme.

So let us gather where the shadows dwell,
In whispers and sighs, let their stories swell.
For in their presence, we are never alone,
In the company of specters, we find our home.